SIDDUR SHABBAT B'YACHAD

A Siddur for Young Children

Edited by Iris Greenbaum and Judith Radousky
Illustrated by Lee Bearson

Siddur Shabbat B'Yachad © 2001 by EKS Publishing Co. Printed in Canada. No part of this book may be transmitted or reproduced by any means, electronic or mechanical, without written permission, except for brief quotations included in critical articles and reviews. For information contact the publisher.

EKS Publishing Co.
P.O. Box 9750, Berkeley, CA 94709-0750
e-mail: EKS@wenet.net
Phone (510) 558-9200 • Fax (510) 558-9255

First Printing, July 2001
ISBN 0-939144-36-0

Acknowledgments

Shabbat B'Yachad, 'Shabbat Together,' was created by parents at Congregation Netivot Shalom in Berkeley, California. This *siddur* is an integral part of the program that parents developed to introduce young children to the *Shabbat* morning prayers.

Special thanks to Rabbi Stuart Kelman, for his wisdom, loving support, and guidance in the creation of *Shabbat B'Yachad*. With Rabbi Kelman's help, we grappled with the liturgy to make it accessible for young children and their families. *Todah Rabbah*.

Sheila Jelen, Lee Bearson, Babbie Freiberg, and Tali Ziv originally conceived of *Shabbat B'Yachad* as a participatory family service. We are particularly grateful to Lee for his inspirational drawings which give depth and beauty to the *t'fillot* in the children's siddur. We also want to thank Peggy Sandel, Judy Massarano, and Carol Dorf for their careful reading of the text and their many helpful comments and ideas. Many thanks to Claudia Valas for her vision and her willingness to make the *Shabbat B'Yachad* experience available to other communities.

Most importantly, we would like to acknowledge all the *Shabbat B'Yachad* families who have created a joyful davening community for families with young children.

"Teach your children in the way they should go and when they are old they will not depart from it."

YIDDISH FOLK SAYING

1

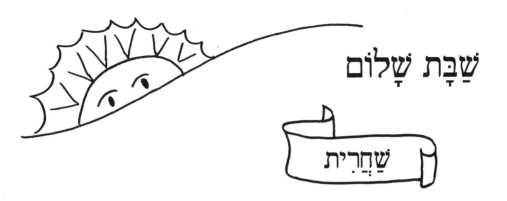

שַׁבָּת שָׁלוֹם

שַׁחֲרִית

מוֹדֶה (מוֹדָה) אֲנִי לְפָנֶיךָ, מֶלֶךְ חַי וְקַיָּם,
שֶׁהֶחֱזַרְתָּ בִּי נִשְׁמָתִי בְּחֶמְלָה רַבָּה אֱמוּנָתֶךָ.

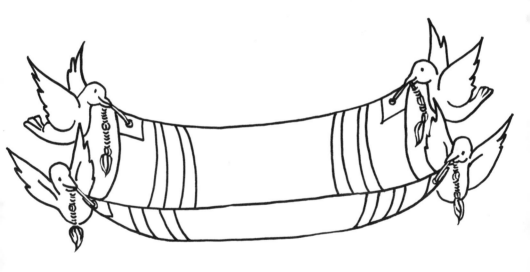

מַה טֹּבוּ אֹהָלֶיךָ יַעֲקֹב,
מִשְׁכְּנֹתֶיךָ יִשְׂרָאֵל.
וַאֲנִי בְּרֹב חַסְדְּךָ אָבוֹא בֵיתֶךָ.

SHABBAT SHALOM

Shacharit • Morning Service

Modeh (female*: Modah) ani l'fanechah, melech chai v'kayam*
Shehechezarta bi nishmati, b'chemlah rabah emunatecha.
Thank you God. You have lovingly given me a new day!

Mah tovu ohalecha Ya'akov, mishkenotecha Yisrael.
How wonderful are your tents children of Israel,
How wonderful are your homes, synagogues, and special
places where you come together.

Va'ani berov chasdecha avo veitecha.
I am full of loving-kindness as I enter into Your house of
prayer.

בָּרוּךְ אַתָּה יְיָ אֱלֹהֵינוּ מֶלֶךְ הָעוֹלָם

...אֲשֶׁר נָתַן לַשֶּׂכְוִי בִינָה, לְהַבְחִין בֵּין יוֹם וּבֵין לָיְלָה.

...שֶׁעָשַׂנִי בְּצַלְמוֹ.

...שֶׁעָשַׂנִי יִשְׂרָאֵל.

...שֶׁעָשַׂנִי בֶּן (בַּת) חוֹרִין.

...פּוֹקֵחַ עִוְרִים.

...מַלְבִּישׁ עֲרֻמִּים.

...מַתִּיר אֲסוּרִים.

...זוֹקֵף כְּפוּפִים.

...רוֹקַע הָאָרֶץ עַל הַמָּיִם.

...שֶׁעָשָׂה לִי כָּל צָרְכִּי.

...הַמֵּכִין מִצְעֲדֵי גָבֶר.

...אוֹזֵר יִשְׂרָאֵל בִּגְבוּרָה.

...עוֹטֵר יִשְׂרָאֵל בְּתִפְאָרָה.

...הַנּוֹתֵן לַיָּעֵף כֹּחַ.

...הַמַּעֲבִיר שֵׁנָה מֵעֵינָי וּתְנוּמָה מֵעַפְעַפָּי.

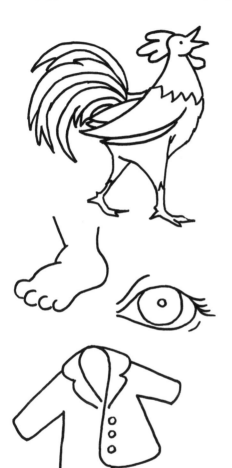

Baruch Atah Adonai Eloheinu melech ha olam . . .

. . . asher natan lasechvi vinah l'havchin bein yom u'vein lailah

. . . she'asani b'tzalmo

. . . she'asani Yisrael

. . . she'asani ben (female: bat) chorin

. . . pokei'ach iv'rim

. . . mal'bish arumim

. . . matir asurim

. . . zokeif k'fufim

. . . roka ha'aretz al hamayim

. . . she'asa li kol tzorki

. . . hameichin mitz'ahdei gaver

. . . ohzeir Yisrael big'vurah

. . . ohteir Yisrael b'tif'arah

. . . hanotein laya'eif ko'ach

. . . hama'avir sheinah mei'ei'nai, u't'numah mei'af'apai

Praised are you Adonai our God, Ruler of the universe . . .

. . . who helps the rooster to know the difference between day and night

. . . who has made me in Your image

. . . who has made me Jewish (add your personal gratitude for who you are, such as a mother, father, brother, sister, good friend, etc.)

. . . who has made me free

. . . who has opened my eyes to see

. . . who has given me clothes to protect me

. . . who helps those who are not free

. . . who gives us strength to hold ourselves up

. . . who creates the solid earth below and the heavens above

. . . who cares for our needs

. . . who guides us throughout the day

. . . who strengthens us with courage

. . . who crowns us with splendor

. . . who gives strength to the tired

. . . who awakens us from our sleep and opens our eyes to a new day.

בָּרוּךְ שֶׁאָמַר

וְהָיָה הָעוֹלָם.

בָּרוּךְ הוּא.

Baruch she'amar v'hayah ha'olam
Praise the One who spoke . . .
and there was the world!

Baruch hu.
Praise Adonai!

הַלְלוּיָהּ.
הַלְלוּ אֵל בְּקָדְשׁוֹ, הַלְלוּהוּ בִּרְקִיעַ עֻזּוֹ.
הַלְלוּהוּ בִּגְבוּרֹתָיו, הַלְלוּהוּ כְּרֹב גֻּדְלוֹ.
הַלְלוּהוּ בְּתֵקַע שׁוֹפָר, הַלְלוּהוּ בְּנֵבֶל וְכִנּוֹר.
הַלְלוּהוּ בְּתֹף וּמָחוֹל, הַלְלוּהוּ בְּמִנִּים וְעֻגָב.
הַלְלוּהוּ בְּצִלְצְלֵי שָׁמַע, הַלְלוּהוּ בְּצִלְצְלֵי תְרוּעָה.
כֹּל הַנְּשָׁמָה תְּהַלֵּל יָהּ הַלְלוּיָהּ.
כֹּל הַנְּשָׁמָה תְּהַלֵּל יָהּ הַלְלוּיָהּ.

8

Hal'luyah

Hal'lu el b'kod'sho, hal'luhu birki'a uzo

Hal'luhu vig'vurotav, hal'luhu k'rov gudlo

Hal'luhu b'teika shofar, hal'luhu b'neivel v'chinor

Hal'luhu b'tof umachol, hal'luhu b'minim v'ugav

Hal'luhu v'tzil'tz'lei shama,
hal'luhu b'tzil'tz'lei t'ru'ah

Kol han'shamah t'haleil Yah hal'luyah
Kol han'shamah t'haleil Yah hal'luyah

Sing praise to Adonai, in God's holy place!
Sing praise to Adonai, who performs wonders!
Sing praise to Adonai, whose power fills the world!
Sing praise, sound the shofar! Strum the harps and violins!
Beat the drums! Play the flutes!
Strike the cymbals! Blast the trumpets!
Sing Praise to Adonai with every breath and all your being!

בָּרְכוּ אֶת יהוה הַמְבוֹרָךְ׃ (Leader)

בָּרוּךְ יהוה הַמְבוֹרָךְ לְעוֹלָם וָעֶד (Group)
בָּרוּךְ יהוה הַמְבוֹרָךְ לְעוֹלָם וָעֶד (Leader)

בָּרוּךְ אַתָּה יהוה אֱלֹהֵינוּ מֶלֶךְ הָעוֹלָם יוֹצֵר אוֹר
וּבוֹרֵא חֹשֶׁךְ עֹשֶׂה שָׁלוֹם וּבוֹרֵא אֶת הַכֹּל.

אוֹר חָדָשׁ עַל צִיּוֹן תָּאִיר וְנִזְכֶּה כֻלָּנוּ מְהֵרָה לְאוֹרוֹ.
בָּרוּךְ אַתָּה יהוה יוֹצֵר הַמְּאוֹרוֹת.

בָּרוּךְ אַתָּה יהוה הַבּוֹחֵר בְּעַמּוֹ יִשְׂרָאֵל בְּאַהֲבָה.

Barchu et Adonai hamevorach. (Leader)
Praise Adonai, the Source of all blessings. (Leader)

Baruch Adonai hamevorach le'olam va'ed. (Group)
Praise Adonai, the Source of all blessings forever and ever.
(Group)

Baruch Adonai hamevorach le'olam va'ed. (Leader)
Praise Adonai, the Source of all blessings forever and ever.
(Leader)

*Baruch ata Adonai Eloheinu melech ha'olam yotzeir or
u'vorei choshech, oseh shalom u'vorei et ha'kol.*
Praised are You Adonai, who protects the world, creates
light and darkness, makes peace and creates all.

Or chadash al tzion ta'ir v'nizkeh chulanu meheirah le'oro.
Shine a light upon all Israel. May we all feel its radiance
and its splendor.

Baruch ata Adonai yotzeir ha'me'orot.
Praised are You Adonai, Creator of all lights.

Baruch ata Adonai habocheir b'amo Yisrael b'ahavah.
Praised are You Adonai, who loves the people of Israel.

שְׁמַע יִשְׂרָאֵל יְהוה
אֱלֹהֵינוּ יְהוה אֶחָד.

בָּרוּךְ שֵׁם כְּבוֹד מַלְכוּתוֹ לְעוֹלָם וָעֶד.

וְאָהַבְתָּ אֵת יְהוה אֱלֹהֶיךָ, בְּכָל-לְבָבְךָ,
וּבְכָל-נַפְשְׁךָ, וּבְכָל-מְאֹדֶךָ. וְהָיוּ הַדְּבָרִים
הָאֵלֶּה, אֲשֶׁר אָנֹכִי מְצַוְּךָ הַיּוֹם, עַל
לְבָבֶךָ. וְשִׁנַּנְתָּם לְבָנֶיךָ, וְדִבַּרְתָּ בָּם
בְּשִׁבְתְּךָ בְּבֵיתֶךָ, וּבְלֶכְתְּךָ בַדֶּרֶךְ
וּבְשָׁכְבְּךָ, וּבְקוּמֶךָ. וּקְשַׁרְתָּם לְאוֹת עַל
יָדֶךָ, וְהָיוּ לְטֹטָפֹת בֵּין עֵינֶיךָ, וּכְתַבְתָּם
עַל מְזֻזוֹת בֵּיתֶךָ וּבִשְׁעָרֶיךָ.

Shema Yisrael Adonai Eloheinu Adonai echad.
Listen all Israel: Adonai, is our God, Adonai is one.

Baruch sheim kevod malchuto l'olam va'ed.
Praised is the name, Protector of the world forever and ever.

V'ahavta et Adonai Elohecha b'chol l'vav'cha uv'chol naf-shecha u'v'chol m'odecha. V'hayu ha'd'varim ha'eileh asher anochi m'tzav'cha hayom al l'vavecha. V'shinan'tam l'vanecha v'dibar'ta bam, b'shiv't'cha b'veitecha u'v'lech'techa va'derech uv'shoch'becha u'v'kumecha. Uk'shar'tam l'ot al yadecha, v'hayu l'totafot bein einecha, uch'tav'tam al m'zuzot beitecha u'vish'arecha.

Love Adonai with all your heart, all your soul and all your strength. Keep God in your heart wherever you go. Teach these words to your children. Talk about these teachings when you are at home or away; when you are awake or when you lie down at night. Tie them on your hand and keep them between your eyes. Write them in the *mezuzot* on your homes and your gates.

אֱמֶת אַתָּה הוּא רִאשׁוֹן.
אֱמֶת אַתָּה הוּא אַחֲרוֹן.
וּמִבַּלְעָדֶיךָ אֵין לָנוּ מֶלֶךְ גּוֹאֵל וּמוֹשִׁיעַ.

Emet emet emet emet
Emet emet emet emet
Emet atah hu rishon.

Emet emet emet emet
Emet emet emet emet
Emet atah hu acharon.

This is true: You are first. You are last.

Umi'bal'adecha ein lanu melech, melech goeil u'moshia.
Umi'bal'adecha ein lanu melech, melech goeil u'moshia.

You are always there to protect us and guide us.

מִי כָמֹכָה
בָּאֵלִם יהוה?

מִי כָּמֹכָה
נֶאְדָּר בַּקֹּדֶשׁ?

נוֹרָא תְהִלֹּת
עֹשֵׂה פֶלֶא.

16

Mi chamocha be'eilim Adonai?
Who is like You, Adonai?

Mi kamocha nedar bakodesh?
Who is like You, in wonder and holiness?

Nora t'hilot osei fele.
You are full of splendor, the maker of miracles!

שִׂים שָׁלוֹם טוֹבָה וּבְרָכָה חֵן וָחֶסֶד
וְרַחֲמִים עָלֵינוּ וְעַל כָּל יִשְׂרָאֵל עַמֶּךָ.

עֹשֶׂה שָׁלוֹם בִּמְרוֹמָיו
הוּא יַעֲשֶׂה שָׁלוֹם עָלֵינוּ
וְעַל כָּל יִשְׂרָאֵל וְאִמְרוּ: אָמֵן.

Amidah

Sim shalom tovah u'vracha, chein va'chesed v'rachamim, aleinu v'al kol Yisrael amecha.

Grant us peace, goodness, blessing, and love. Show your compassion to us and all of Israel.

Oseh shalom bim'romav, hu ya'aseh shalom, aleinu v'al kol Yisrael, v'imru, amen.

May the One who creates peace in the Universe, grant peace and loving kindness to us and all of Israel. And let us say, Amen.

קְרִיאַת הַתּוֹרָה

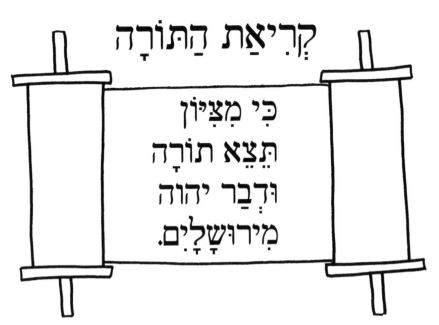

כִּי מִצִּיּוֹן
תֵּצֵא תוֹרָה
וּדְבַר יְהוה
מִירוּשָׁלָיִם.

בָּרוּךְ שֶׁנָּתַן תּוֹרָה לְעַמּוֹ
יִשְׂרָאֵל בִּקְדֻשָּׁתוֹ.

שְׁמַע יִשְׂרָאֵל יהוה אֱלֹהֵינוּ יהוה אֶחָד.

אֶחָד אֱלֹהֵינוּ, גָּדוֹל אֲדוֹנֵנוּ, קָדוֹשׁ שְׁמוֹ.

גַּדְּלוּ לַיהוה אִתִּי, וּנְרוֹמְמָה שְׁמוֹ יַחְדָּו.

K'riat haTorah • Torah Service

Ki mi'tzion teitzei Torah u'd'var Adonai mi'rushalayim.
From Israel, the Torah shines. From Jerusalem, all of God's
words spread.

Baruch shenatan Torah, Torah, l'amo Yisrael bik'dushato.
Praise God, in Your holiness, You gave us Your Torah.

Shema Yisrael Adonai Eloheinu Adonai echad.
Listen all Israel: Adonai is our God, Adonai is One.

Echad Eloheinu, gadol Adoneinu, kadosh shemo.
Our God is one. Our God is great. God's name is holy.

Gadlu ladonai iti, u'neromema shemo yachdav.
Sing out God's greatness with me!
Together, we honor God's name!

תּוֹרָה צִוָּה לָנוּ מֹשֶׁה
מוֹרָשָׁה קְהִלַּת יַעֲקֹב.

עֵץ חַיִּים הִיא
לַמַּחֲזִיקִים בָּהּ
וְתֹמְכֶיהָ מְאֻשָּׁר.

22

Torah tzivah lanu Moshe, morasha k'hilat Ya'akov.

This is the Torah given to Moses our teacher, for us to follow. It is our heritage as the community of Israel.

Eitz chayyim hi la'machazikim ba, v'tom'chehah m'ushar.

It is a tree of life for those who hold fast to it, and all its supporters are happy.

אֵין כָּאדוֹנֵינוּ   אֵין כֵּאלֹהֵינוּ
אֵין כְּמוֹשִׁיעֵנוּ.   אֵין כְּמַלְכֵּנוּ

מִי כָאדוֹנֵינוּ   מִי כֵאלֹהֵינוּ
מִי כְמוֹשִׁיעֵנוּ.   מִי כְמַלְכֵּנוּ

נוֹדֶה לַאדוֹנֵינוּ   נוֹדֶה לֵאלֹהֵינוּ
נוֹדֶה לְמוֹשִׁיעֵנוּ.   נוֹדֶה לְמַלְכֵּנוּ

בָּרוּךְ אֲדוֹנֵינוּ   בָּרוּךְ אֱלֹהֵינוּ
בָּרוּךְ מוֹשִׁיעֵנוּ.   בָּרוּךְ מַלְכֵּנוּ

אַתָּה הוּא אֲדוֹנֵינוּ   אַתָּה הוּא אֱלֹהֵינוּ
אַתָּה הוּא מוֹשִׁיעֵנוּ   אַתָּה הוּא מַלְכֵּנוּ

אַתָּה הוּא שֶׁהִקְטִירוּ אֲבוֹתֵינוּ לְפָנֶיךָ אֶת קְטֹרֶת הַסַּמִּים.

Concluding Service

Ein keiloheinu
Ein k'malkeinu

Ein kadoneinu
Ein k'moshi'einu

Mi cheiloheinu
Mi ch'malkeinu

Mi chadoneinu
Mi ch'moshi'einu

Nodeh leiloheinu
Nodeh l'malkeinu

Nodeh ladoneinu
Nodeh l'moshi'einu

Baruch Eloheinu
Baruch malkeinu

Baruch Adoneinu
Baruch moshi'einu

Atah hu Eloheinu
Atah hu malkeinu

Atah hu Adoneinu
Atah hu moshi'einu

Atah hu shehik'tiru avoteinu l'fanecha et k'toret ha'samim.

None compares to You Our God.
None compares to You Our Adonai.
None compares to You Our Majesty.
None compares to You Our Protector.

Who is like You Our God? . . . Adonai?
Who is like You Our Majesty? . . . Protector?

Thank You Our God . . . Adonai
Thank You Our Majesty . . . Protector

Praised are You Our God . . . Adonai
Praised are You Our Majesty . . . Protector

You are Our God . . . Adonai
You are Our Majesty . . . Protector

You are the One to whom our ancestors gave their sweet offerings.

עָלֵינוּ לְשַׁבֵּחַ לַאֲדוֹן הַכֹּל, לָתֵת גְּדֻלָּה לְיוֹצֵר בְּרֵאשִׁית,
שֶׁלֹּא עָשָׂנוּ כְּגוֹיֵי הָאֲרָצוֹת וְלֹא שָׂמָנוּ כְּמִשְׁפְּחוֹת הָאֲדָמָה,
שֶׁלֹּא שָׂם חֶלְקֵנוּ כָּהֶם וְגוֹרָלֵנוּ כְּכָל הֲמוֹנָם.

וַאֲנַחְנוּ כּוֹרְעִים וּמִשְׁתַּחֲוִים וּמוֹדִים
לִפְנֵי מֶלֶךְ, מַלְכֵי הַמְּלָכִים, הַקָּדוֹשׁ בָּרוּךְ הוּא.

אֲדוֹן עוֹלָם אֲשֶׁר מָלַךְ   בְּטֶרֶם כָּל יְצִיר נִבְרָא.
לְעֵת נַעֲשָׂה בְחֶפְצוֹ כֹּל   אֲזַי מֶלֶךְ שְׁמוֹ נִקְרָא.

וְאַחֲרֵי כִּכְלוֹת הַכֹּל   לְבַדּוֹ יִמְלוֹךְ נוֹרָא.
וְהוּא הָיָה וְהוּא הֹוֶה   וְהוּא יִהְיֶה בְּתִפְאָרָה.
וְהוּא אֶחָד וְאֵין שֵׁנִי   לְהַמְשִׁיל לוֹ לְהַחְבִּירָה.
בְּלִי רֵאשִׁית בְּלִי תַכְלִית   וְלוֹ הָעֹז וְהַמִּשְׂרָה.
וְהוּא אֵלִי וְחַי גּוֹאֲלִי   וְצוּר חֶבְלִי בְּעֵת צָרָה.
וְהוּא נִסִּי וּמָנוֹס לִי   מְנָת כּוֹסִי בְּיוֹם אֶקְרָא.
בְּיָדוֹ אַפְקִיד רוּחִי   בְּעֵת אִישַׁן וְאָעִירָה.
וְעִם רוּחִי גְּוִיָּתִי   יְהֹוָה לִי וְלֹא אִירָא.

Aleinu l'shabeiach la'adon ha'kol, latet gedulah le'yotzeir b'reisheet, shelo asanu ke'goyei ha'aratzot, ve'lo samanu k'mish'p'chot ha'adamah, shelo sam chelkeinu ka'hem v'goraleinu k'chol ha'monam.

We join together to praise the Creator of all. You have given us special ways to show our closeness to You.

Va'anachnu korim u'mishtachavim u'modim, lifnei melech malchei ham'lachim, ha'kadosh baruch hu.

We bend our knees and bow to give you our thanks, Majesty of all Majesties. We praise the Holy One.

Adon olam asher malach   b'terem kol y'tzir nivra
L'eit na'asah b'cheftzo kol   azai melech sh'mo nikra

V'acharei kichlot ha'kol   L'vado yimloch nora
V'hu hayah v'hu hoveh   v'hu yi'hi'yeh b'tif'arah

V'hu echad v'ein sheini   l'hamshil lo l'hachbirah
B'li rei'sheet b'li tachlit   v'lo ha'oz v'hamisrah

V'hu eili v'chai go'ali   v'tzur chevli b'eit tzarah
V'hu nisi u'manos li   m'nat kosi b'yom ekra

B'yado afkid ruchi   b'eit ishan v'a'irah
V'im ruchi g'viyati   Adonai li v'lo ira

God, You created all, and You watch over all.
You always were, always are, and will always be.
You are One, there is no other like You,
You watch over me and protect me
You take care of me when I sleep and when I wake
You are with me so I will not be afraid.

וְשָׁמְרוּ בְנֵי יִשְׂרָאֵל
אֶת הַשַּׁבָּת לַעֲשׂוֹת אֶת הַשַּׁבָּת
לְדֹרֹתָם בְּרִית עוֹלָם.

בָּרוּךְ אַתָּה יהוה
אֱלֹהֵינוּ מֶלֶךְ הָעוֹלָם
בּוֹרֵא פְּרִי הַגָּפֶן.

בָּרוּךְ אַתָּה יהוה אֱלֹהֵינוּ
מֶלֶךְ הָעוֹלָם אֲשֶׁר קִדְּשָׁנוּ
בְּמִצְוֹתָיו וְצִוָּנוּ עַל נְטִילַת יָדָיִם.

בָּרוּךְ אַתָּה יהוה אֱלֹהֵינוּ מֶלֶךְ
הָעוֹלָם הַמּוֹצִיא לֶחֶם מִן הָאָרֶץ.

28

Kiddush

V'shamru venei Yisrael et ha'shabat, la'asot et ha'shabat le'doratam berit olam.

The people of Israel promise to make Shabbat special and celebrate Shabbat forever and ever.

Baruch atah Adonai, Eloheinu melech ha'olam, borei p'ri ha'gafen.

Praised are you Adonai our God, Ruler of the universe, who creates the fruit of the vine.

Blessings Before a Meal

Hand washing:

Baruch atah Adonai Eloheinu melech ha'olam, asher kid'shanu b'mitzvatov v'tzivanu al n'tilat ya'dayim.

Praised are you Adonai our God, Ruler of the universe who has given us the special mitzvah of washing hands.

Bread:

Baruch atah Adonai Eloheinu melech ha'olam, ha'motzi lechem min ha'aretz.

Praised are you Adonai our God, Ruler of the universe who brings forth bread from the earth.

Blessings Before a Snack

Foods (other than bread) prepared from grains:

לְהֵינוּ מֶלֶךְ הָעוֹלָם
י מְזוֹנוֹת.

Baruch atah Adonai Eloheinu melech ha'olam, borei minei mezonot.

Praised are you Adonai our God, Ruler of the universe who creates foods to nourish us.

Fruit of the tree:

בָּרוּךְ אַתָּה יהוה אֱלֹהֵינוּ מֶלֶךְ הָעוֹלָם
בּוֹרֵא פְּרִי הָעֵץ.

Baruch atah Adonai Eloheinu melech ha'olam, borei p'ri ha'eitz.

Praised are you Adonai our God, Ruler of the universe who creates the fruit of the tree.

Fruit of the earth:

בָּרוּךְ אַתָּה יהוה אֱלֹהֵינוּ מֶלֶךְ הָעוֹלָם
בּוֹרֵא פְּרִי הָאֲדָמָה.

Baruch atah Adonai Eloheinu melech ha'olam, borei p'ri ha'adamah.

Praised are you Adonai our God, Ruler of the universe who creates the fruit of the earth.

Other food and drinks:

בָּרוּךְ אַתָּה יהוה אֱלֹהֵינוּ מֶלֶךְ הָעוֹלָם
שֶׁהַכֹּל נִהְיֶה בִּדְבָרוֹ.

Baruch atah Adonai Eloheinu melech ha'olam, sheha'kol nihyeh bid'varo.

Praised are you Adonai our God, Ruler of the universe who creates all food and drinks.